GRAPHIC LIBRARY

GRAPHIC HISTORY

THE BOSTON MASSACRE

by Michael Burgan
illustrated by Bob Wiacek,
Keith Williams, and
Charles Barnett III

Consultant:
Susan Goganian, Site Director
The Bostonian Society
Boston, Massachusetts

Capstone press

Mankato, Minnesota

Graphic Library is published by Capstone Press,
151 Good Counsel Drive, P.O. Box 669, Mankato, Minnesota 56002.
www.capstonepress.com

Printed in the United States of America

1 2 3 4 5 6 10 09 08 07 06 05

Library of Congress Cataloging-in-Publication Data
Burgan, Michael.
The Boston Massacre / by Michael Burgan; illustrated by Bob Wiacek, Keith Williams, and Charles Barnett III.
p. cm.—(Graphic library. Graphic history)
Includes bibliographical references and index.
ISBN 0-7368-4368-X (hardcover)
ISBN 0-7368-6202-1 (softcover)
1. Boston Massacre, 1770—Juvenile literature. I. Title. II. Series.
E215.4.B869 2006
973.3'113—dc22 2005006462

Summary: In graphic novel format, tells the story of the Boston Massacre.

Art and Editorial Direction
Jason Knudson and Blake A. Hoena

Designers
Jason Knudson and Ted Williams

Colorist
Brent Schoonover

Editor
Erika L. Shores

Editor's note: Direct quotations from primary sources are indicated by a yellow background.

Direct quotations appear on the following pages:
Pages 8, 13, 14, 19, 20, 26, from *The Boston Massacre* by Hiller B. Zobel (New York: W. W. Norton, 1970).
Page 10, from *Samuel Adams: The Fateful Years, 1764–1776* by Stewart Beach (New York: Dodd, Mead, and Company, 1965).
Page 25 (top), from *John Adams and the American Revolution* by Catherine Drinker Bowen (Boston: Little, Brown, and Company, 1950).
Page 25 (bottom), from John Adams' speech at the Boston Massacre trial (The Boston Massacre Historical Society, www.bostonmassacre.net/trial/acct-adams3.htm).

TABLE OF CONTENTS

CHAPTER 1

TROOPS COME TO BOSTON

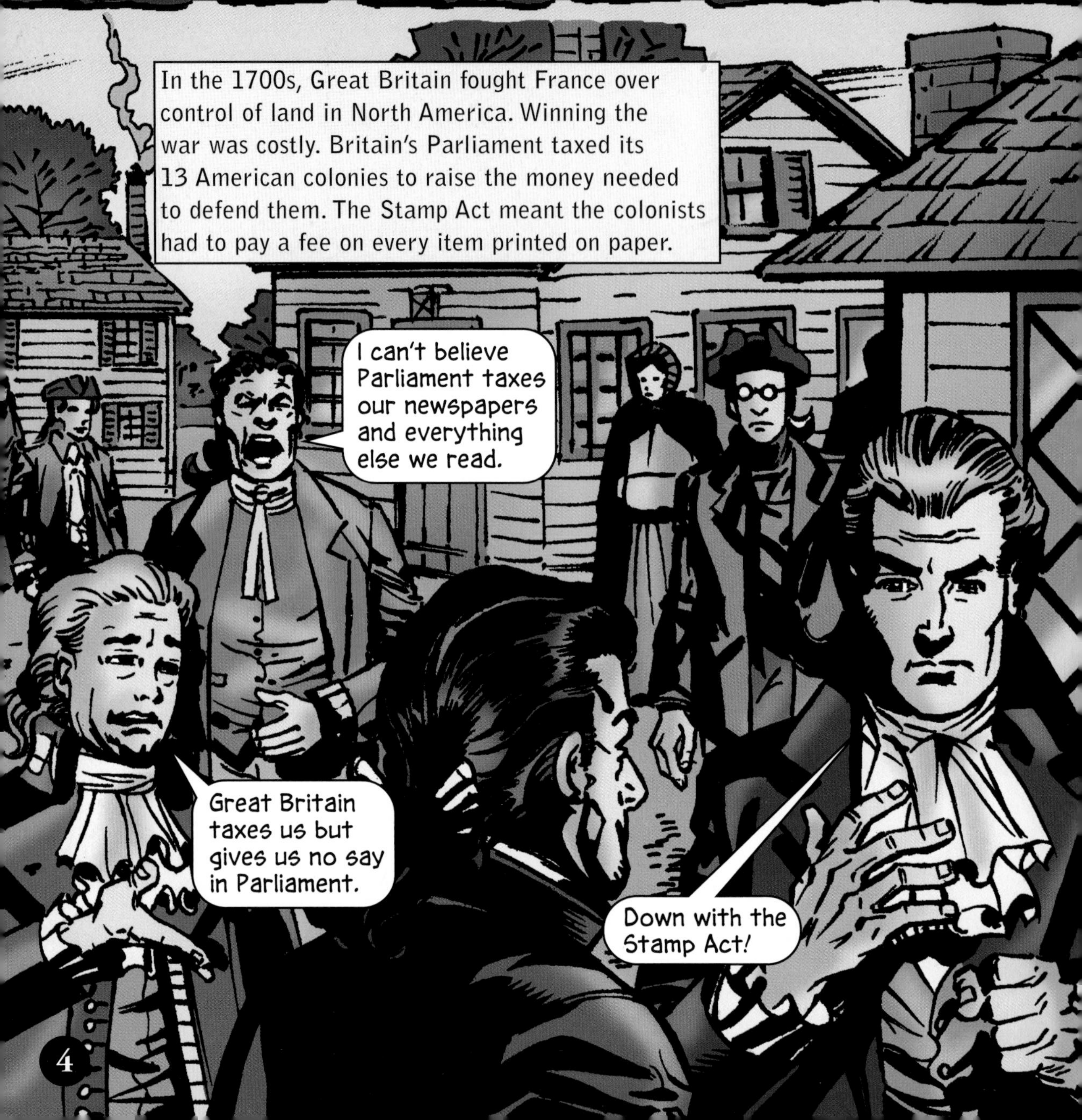
In the 1700s, Great Britain fought France over control of land in North America. Winning the war was costly. Britain's Parliament taxed its 13 American colonies to raise the money needed to defend them. The Stamp Act meant the colonists had to pay a fee on every item printed on paper.
I can't believe Parliament taxes our newspapers and everything else we read.
Great Britain taxes us but gives us no say in Parliament.
Down with the Stamp Act!

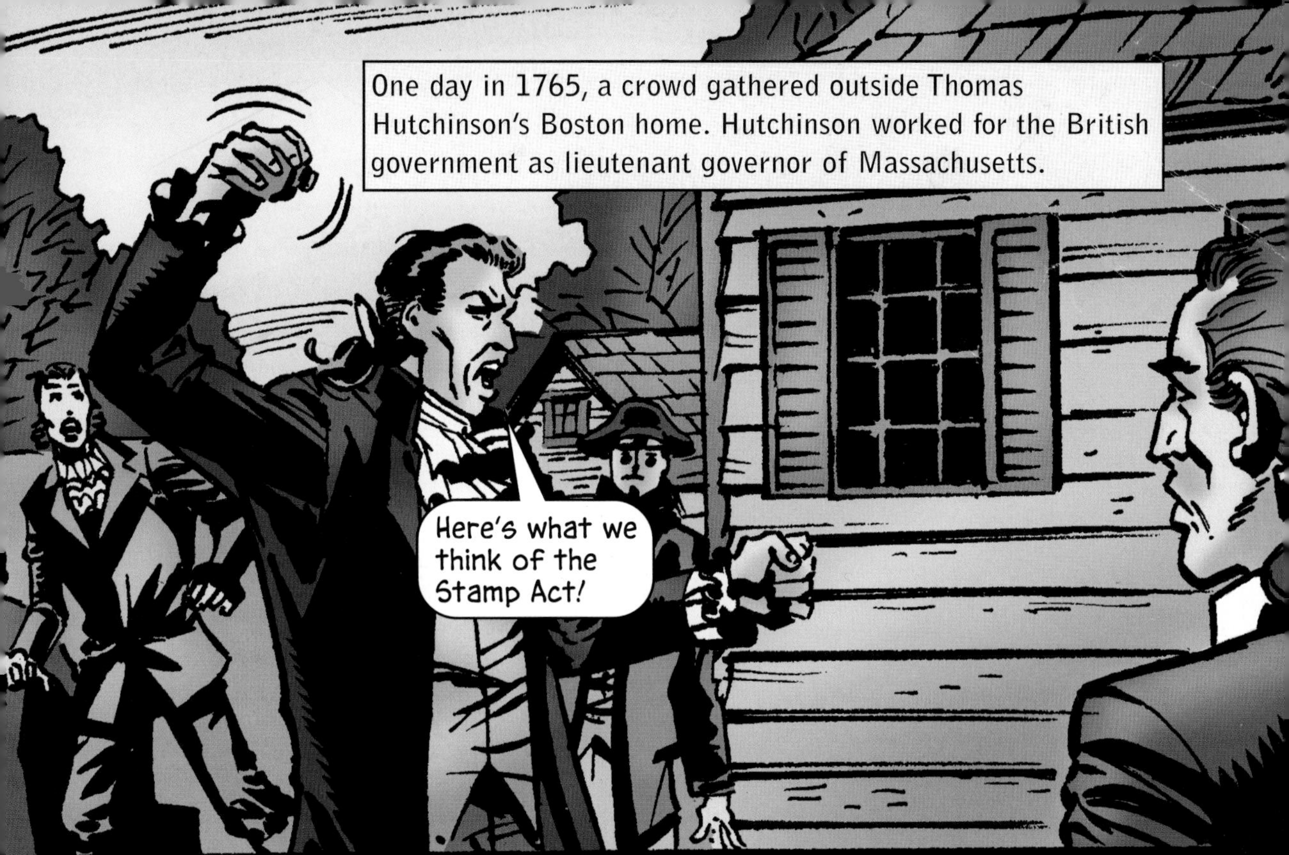
One day in 1765, a crowd gathered outside Thomas Hutchinson's Boston home. Hutchinson worked for the British government as lieutenant governor of Massachusetts.
Here's what we think of the Stamp Act!

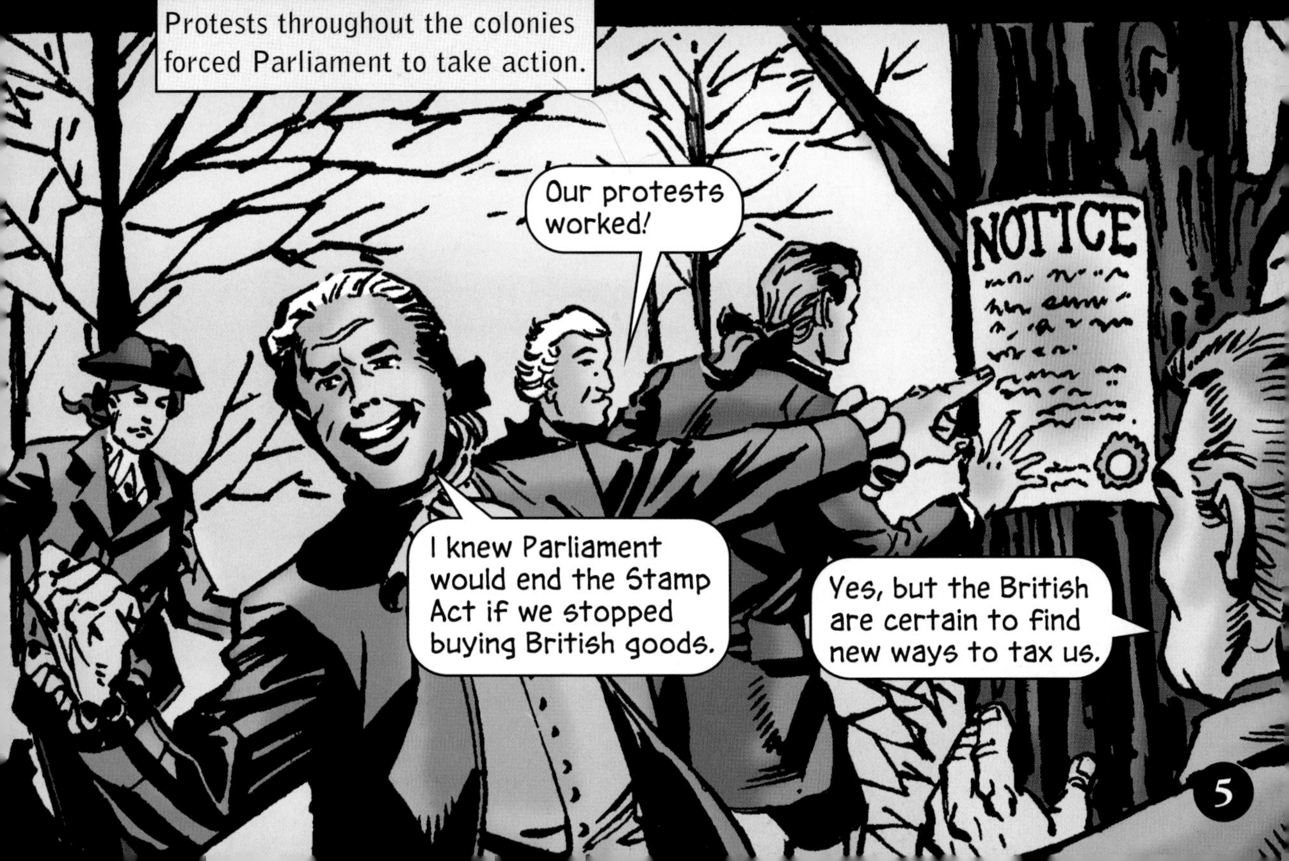
Protests throughout the colonies forced Parliament to take action.
Our protests worked!
NOTICE
I knew Parliament would end the Stamp Act if we stopped buying British goods.
Yes, but the British are certain to find new ways to tax us.

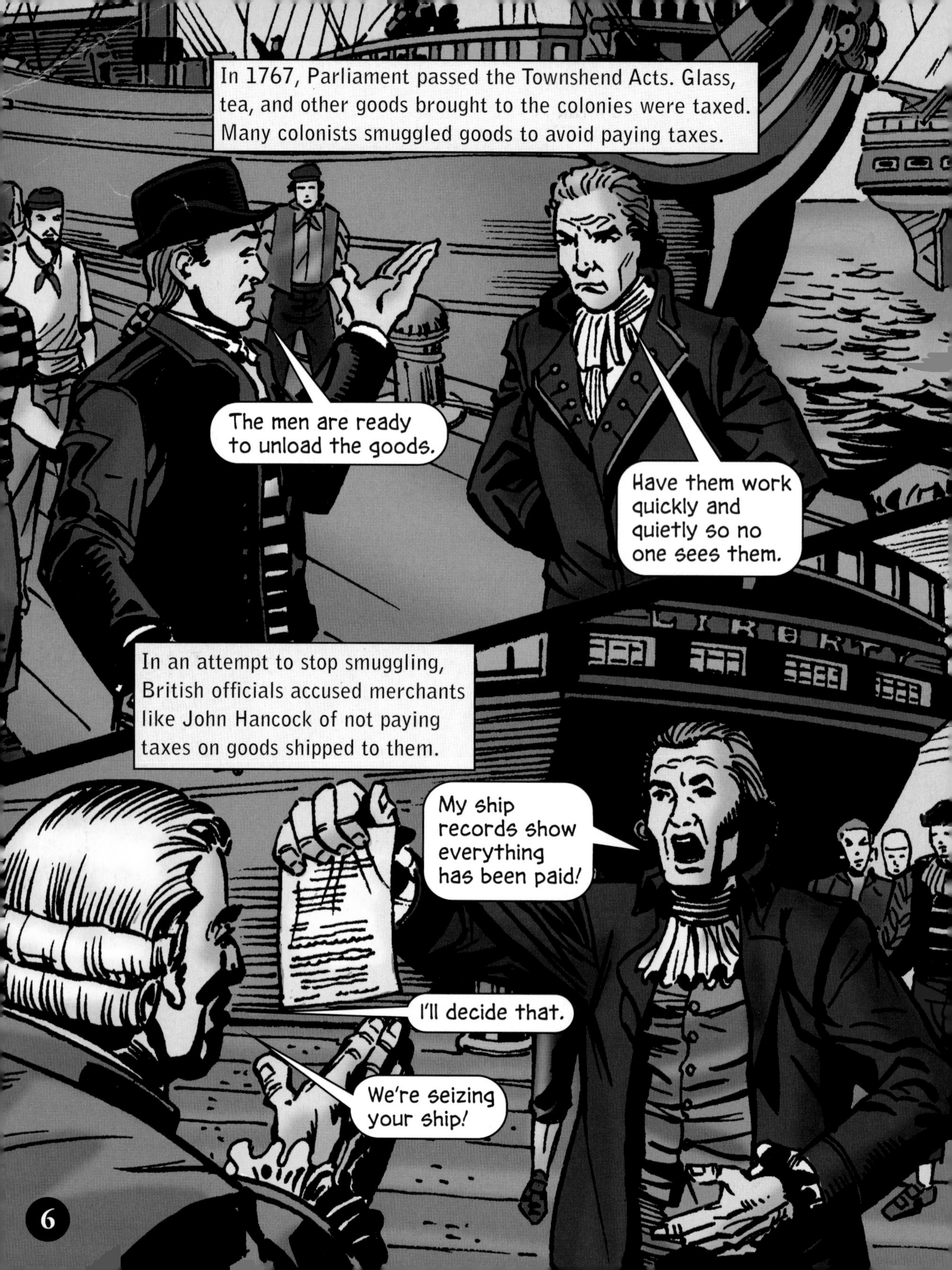
In 1767, Parliament passed the Townshend Acts. Glass, tea, and other goods brought to the colonies were taxed. Many colonists smuggled goods to avoid paying taxes.
The men are ready to unload the goods.
Have them work quickly and quietly so no one sees them.
In an attempt to stop smuggling, British officials accused merchants like John Hancock of not paying taxes on goods shipped to them.
My ship records show everything has been paid!
I'll decide that.
We're seizing your ship!

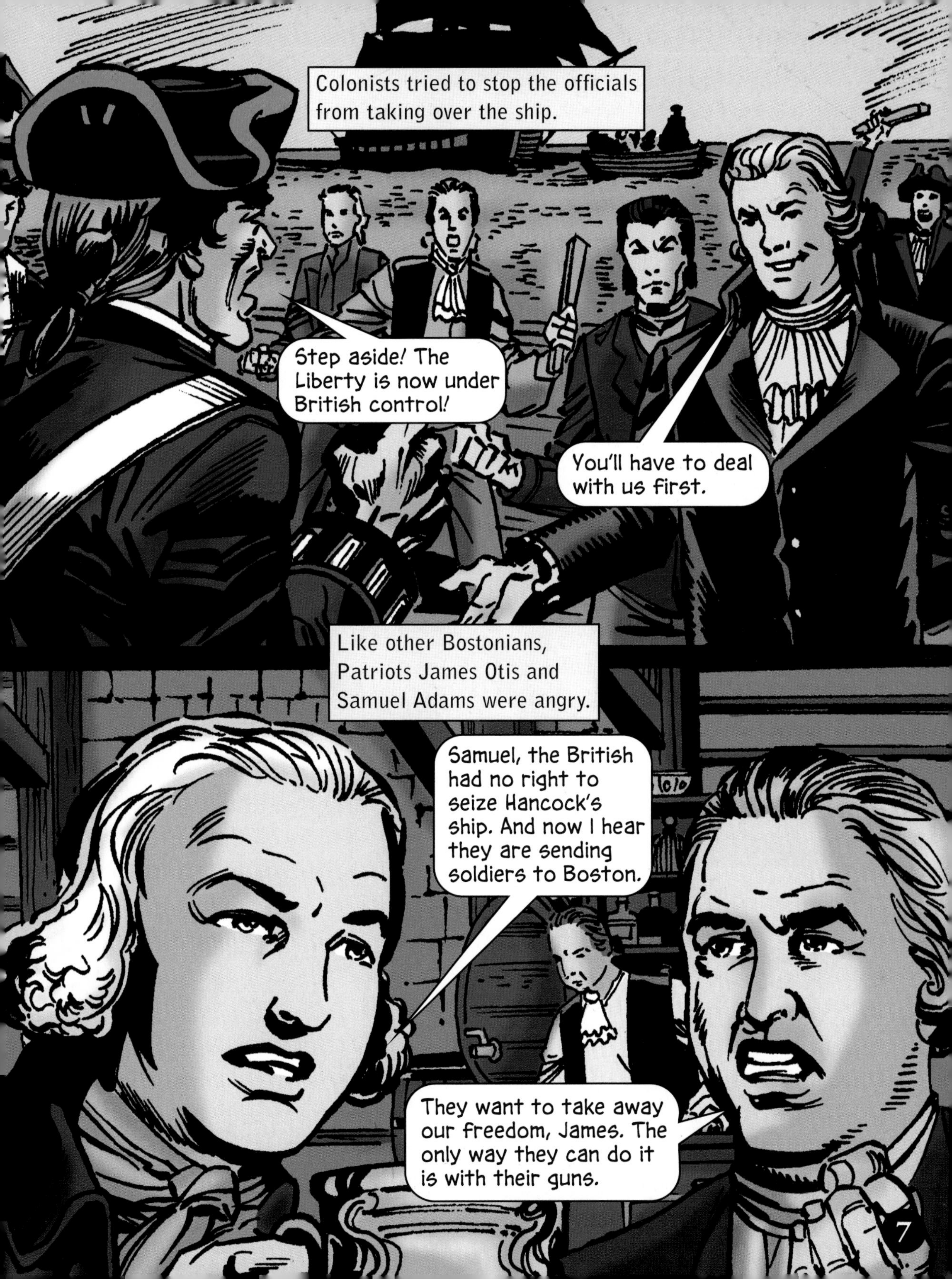

Colonists tried to stop the officials from taking over the ship.
Step aside! The Liberty is now under British control!
You'll have to deal with us first.
Like other Bostonians, Patriots James Otis and Samuel Adams were angry.
Samuel, the British had no right to seize Hancock's ship. And now I hear they are sending soldiers to Boston.
They want to take away our freedom, James. The only way they can do it is with their guns.

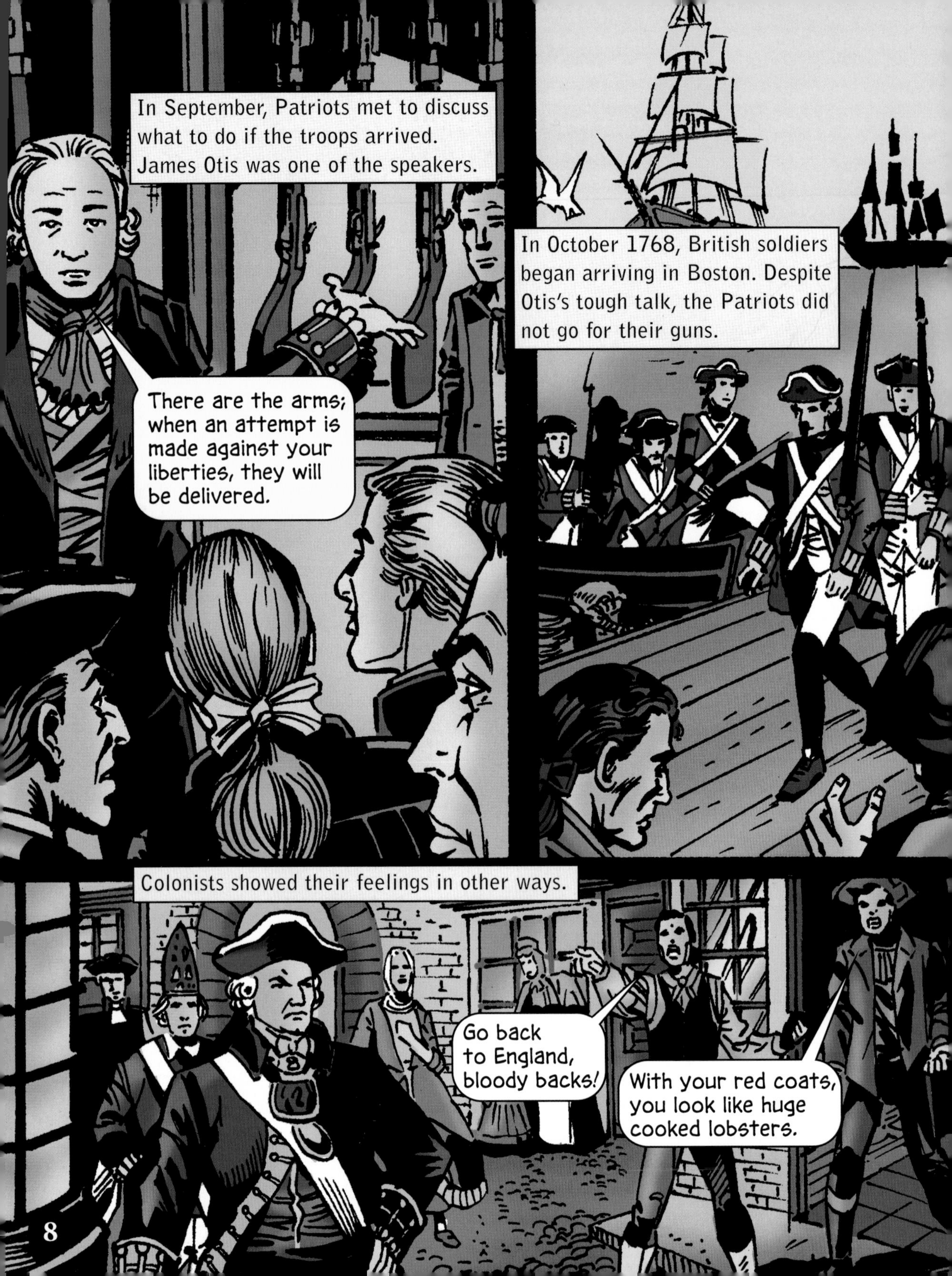
In September, Patriots met to discuss what to do if the troops arrived. James Otis was one of the speakers.
There are the arms; when an attempt is made against your liberties, they will be delivered.
In October 1768, British soldiers began arriving in Boston. Despite Otis's tough talk, the Patriots did not go for their guns.
Colonists showed their feelings in other ways.
Go back to England, bloody backs!
With your red coats, you look like huge cooked lobsters.

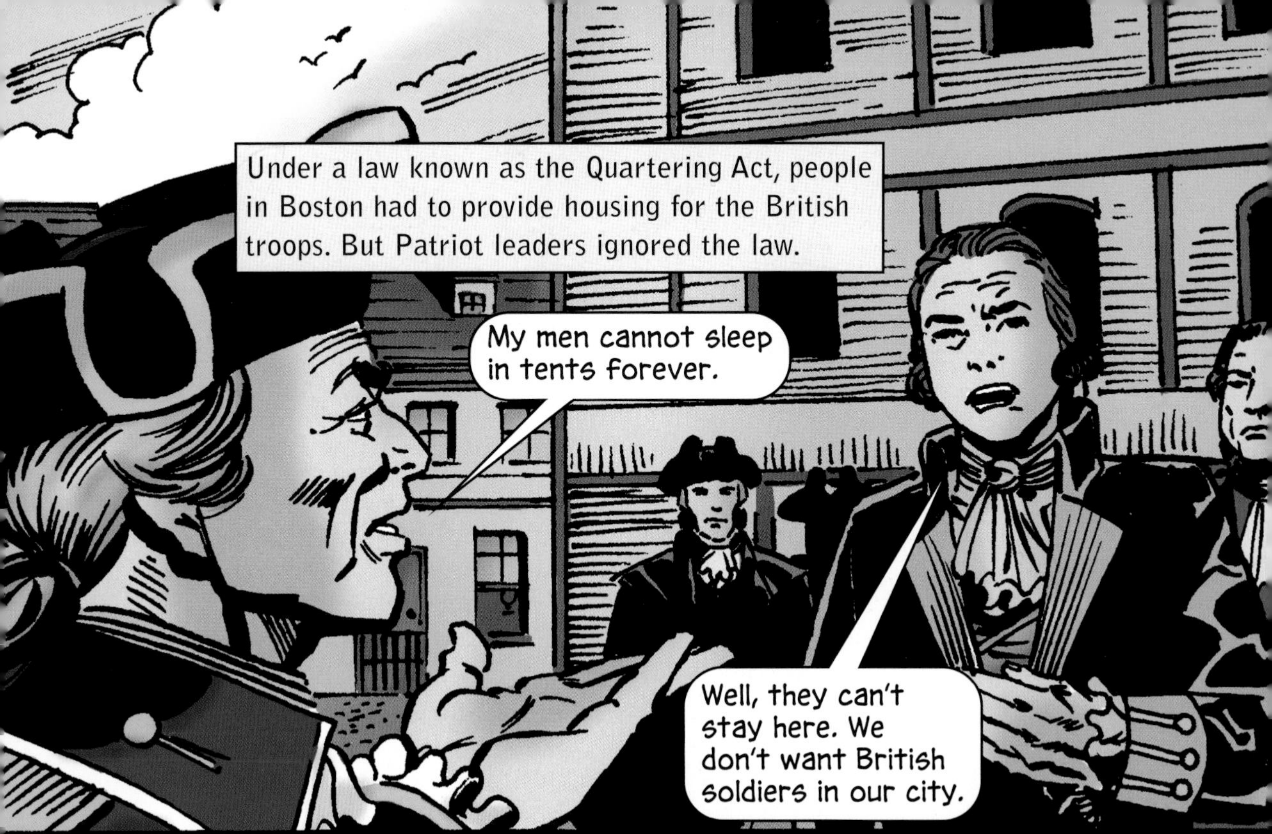
Under a law known as the Quartering Act, people in Boston had to provide housing for the British troops. But Patriot leaders ignored the law.
My men cannot sleep in tents forever.
Well, they can't stay here. We don't want British soldiers in our city.

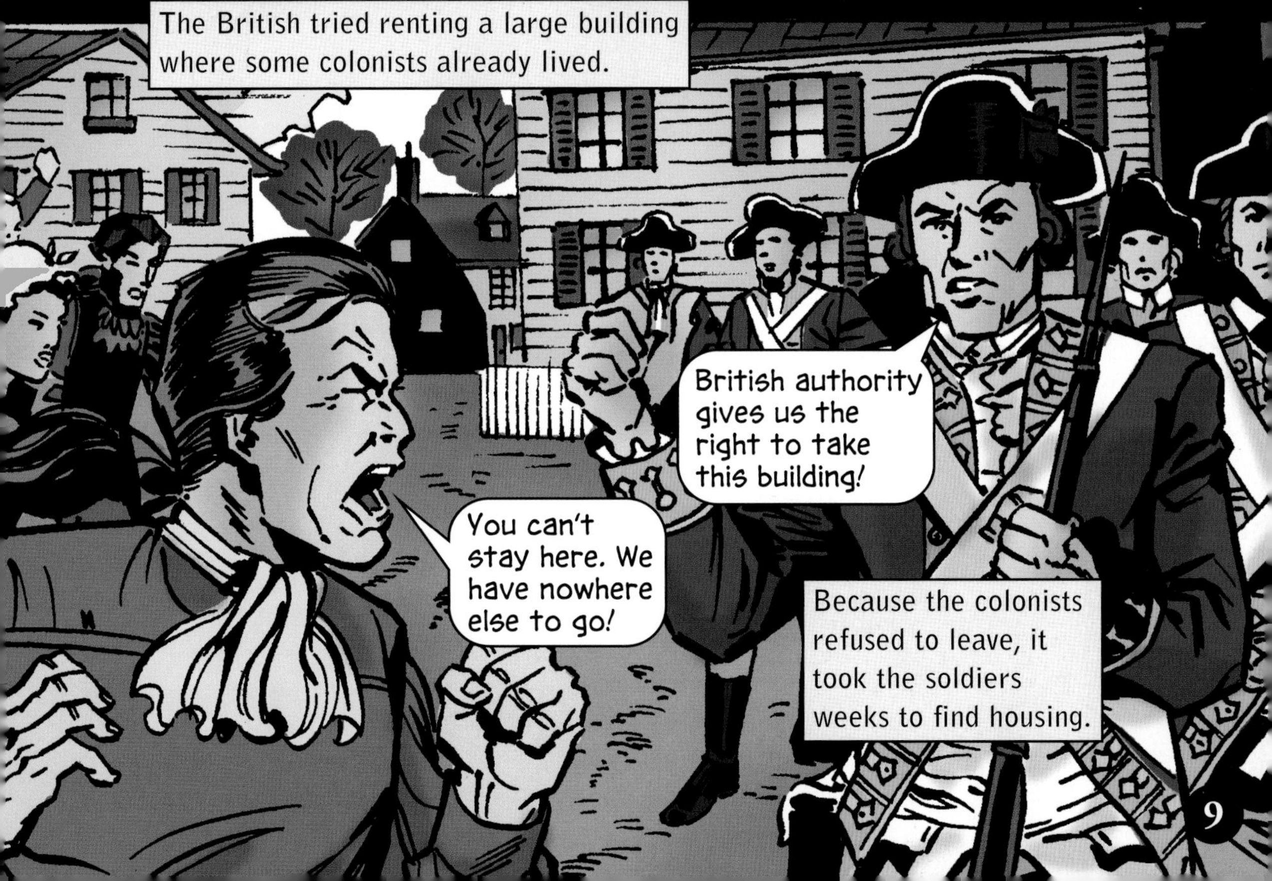
The British tried renting a large building where some colonists already lived.
British authority gives us the right to take this building!
You can't stay here. We have nowhere else to go!
Because the colonists refused to leave, it took the soldiers weeks to find housing.

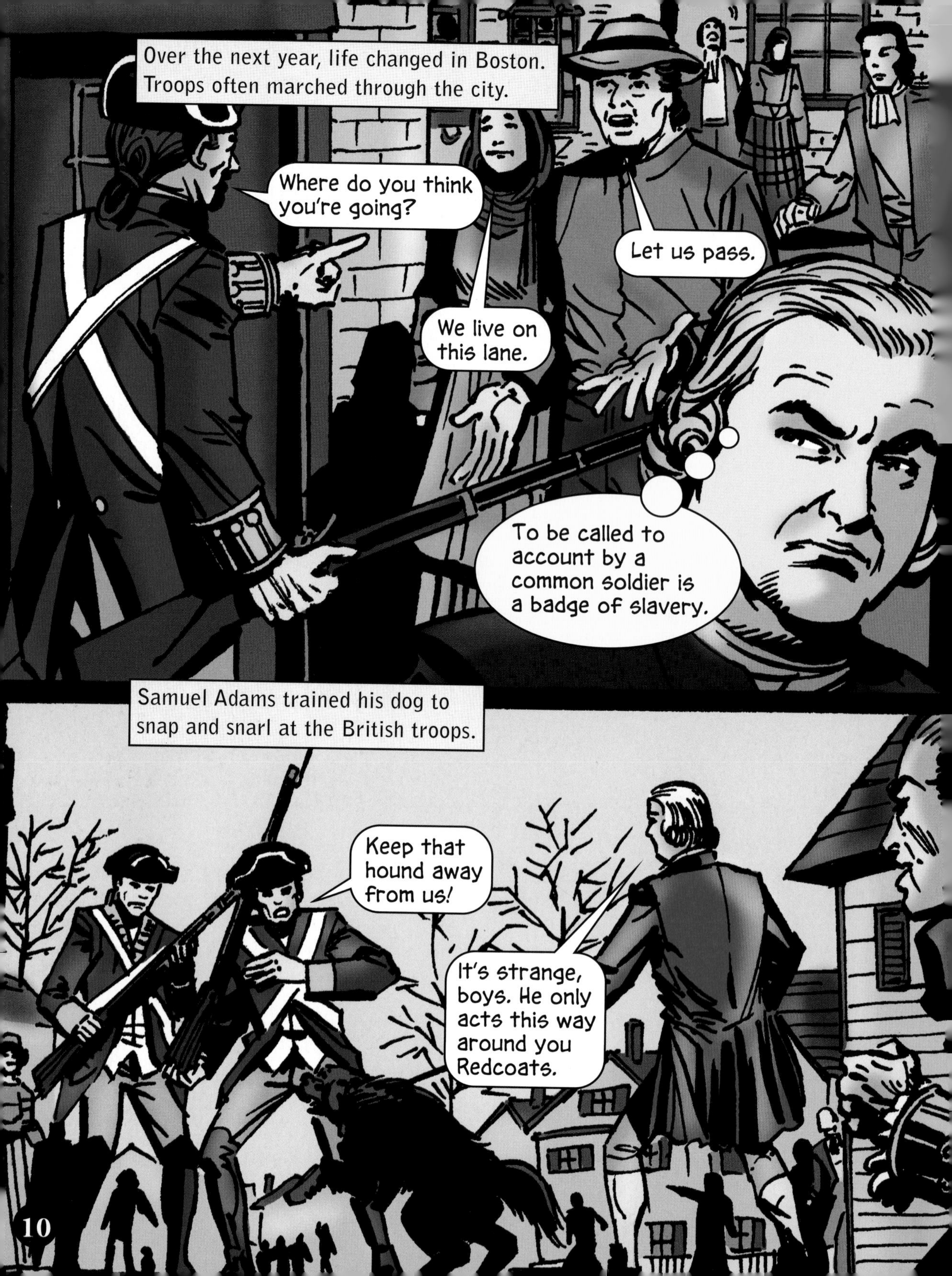
Over the next year, life changed in Boston. Troops often marched through the city.
Where do you think you're going?
We live on this lane.
Let us pass.
To be called to account by a common soldier is a badge of slavery.
Samuel Adams trained his dog to snap and snarl at the British troops.
Keep that hound away from us!
It's strange, boys. He only acts this way around you Redcoats.

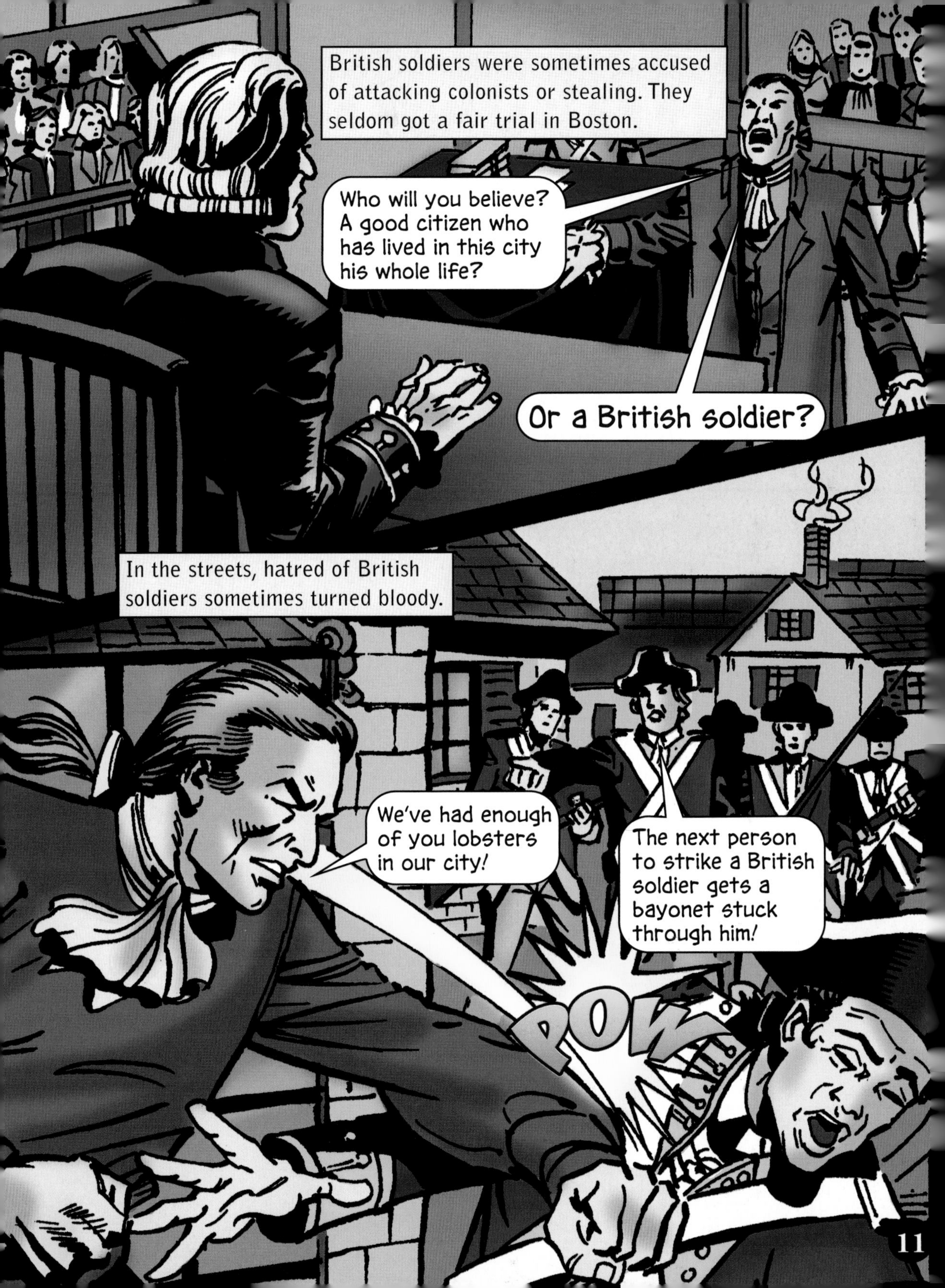
British soldiers were sometimes accused of attacking colonists or stealing. They seldom got a fair trial in Boston.
Who will you believe? A good citizen who has lived in this city his whole life?
Or a British soldier?
In the streets, hatred of British soldiers sometimes turned bloody.
We've had enough of you lobsters in our city!
The next person to strike a British soldier gets a bayonet stuck through him!
POW

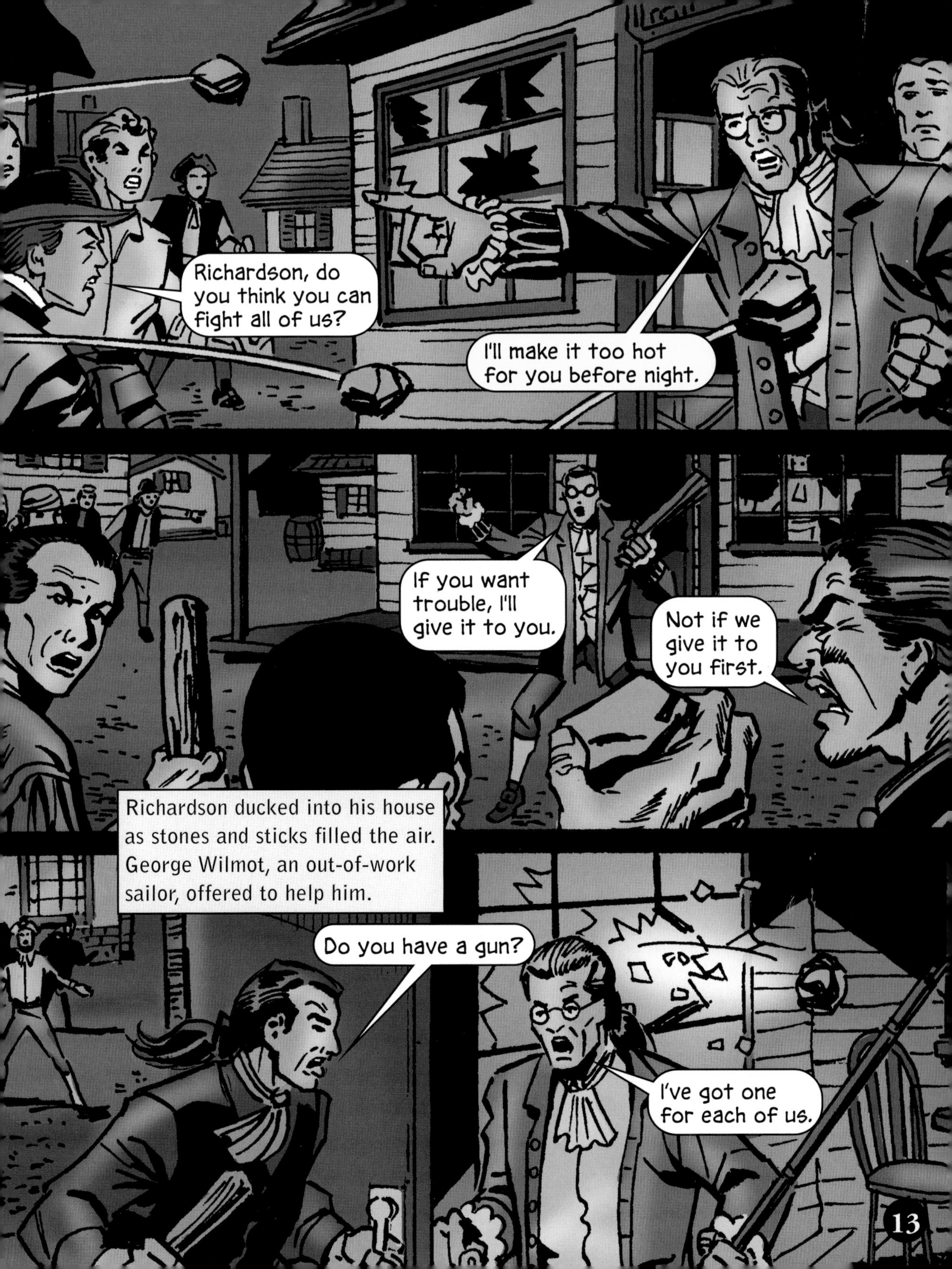
Richardson, do you think you can fight all of us?
I'll make it too hot for you before night.
If you want trouble, I'll give it to you.
Not if we give it to you first.
Richardson ducked into his house as stones and sticks filled the air. George Wilmot, an out-of-work sailor, offered to help him.
Do you have a gun?
I've got one for each of us.

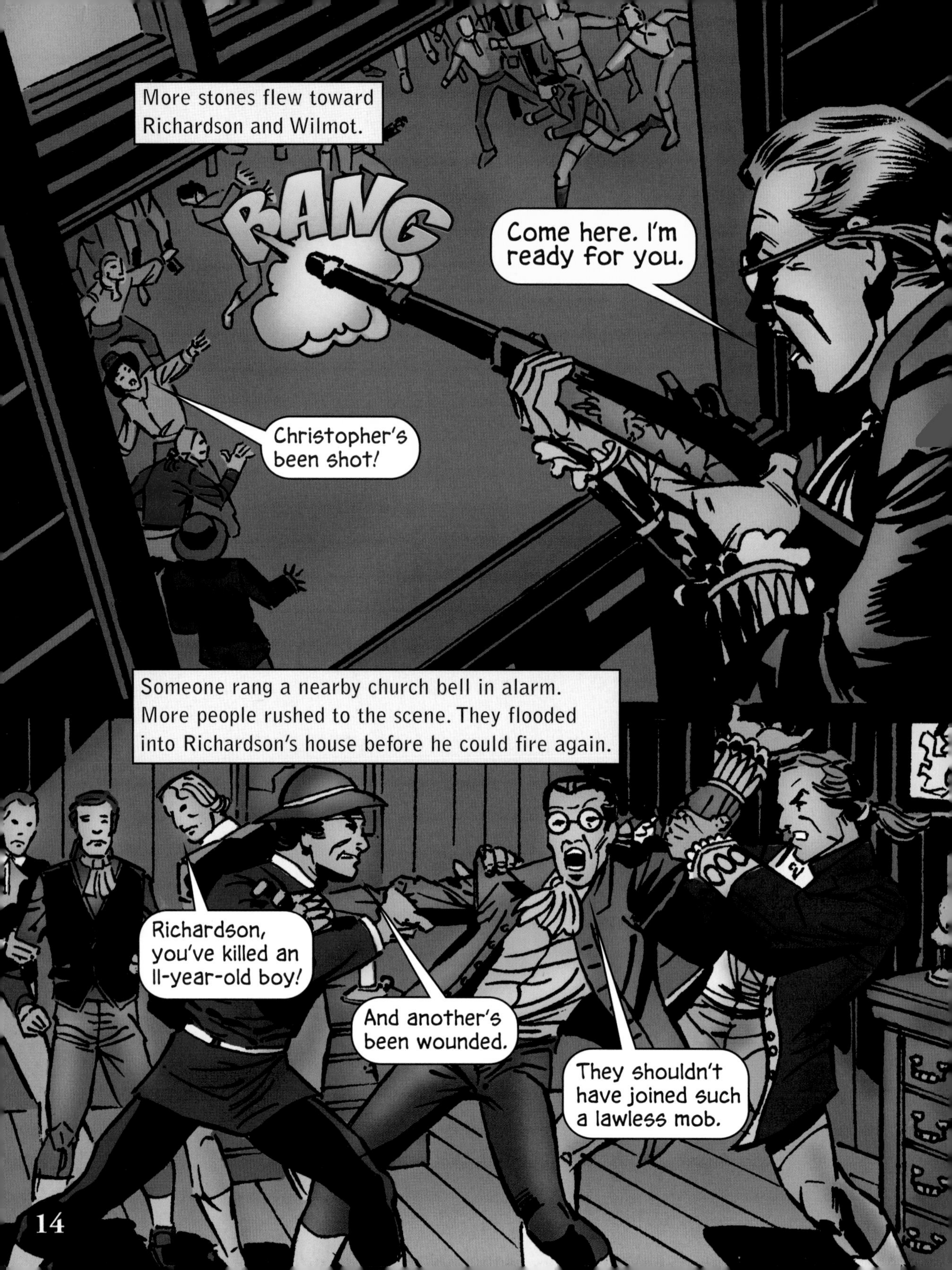
More stones flew toward Richardson and Wilmot.
BANG
Come here. I'm ready for you.
Christopher's been shot!
Someone rang a nearby church bell in alarm. More people rushed to the scene. They flooded into Richardson's house before he could fire again.
Richardson, you've killed an 11-year-old boy!
And another's been wounded.
They shouldn't have joined such a lawless mob.

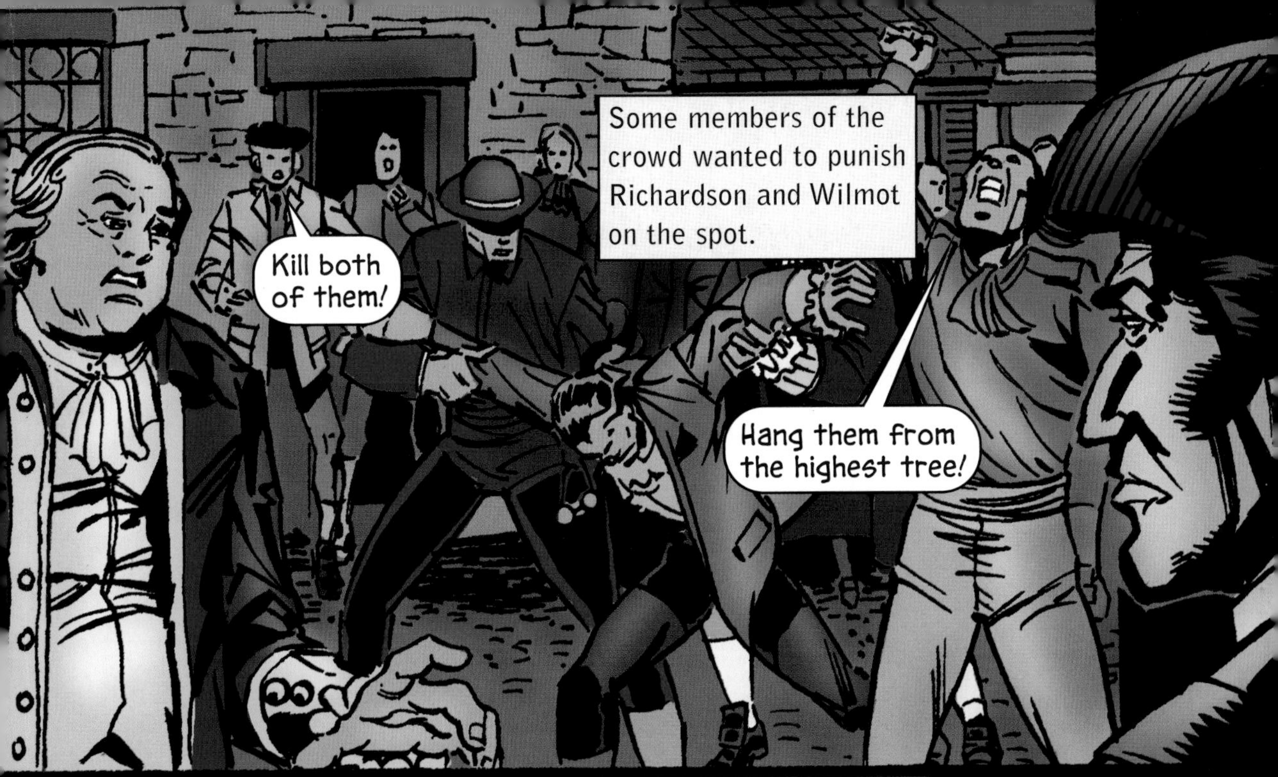
Some members of the crowd wanted to punish Richardson and Wilmot on the spot.
Kill both of them!
Hang them from the highest tree!

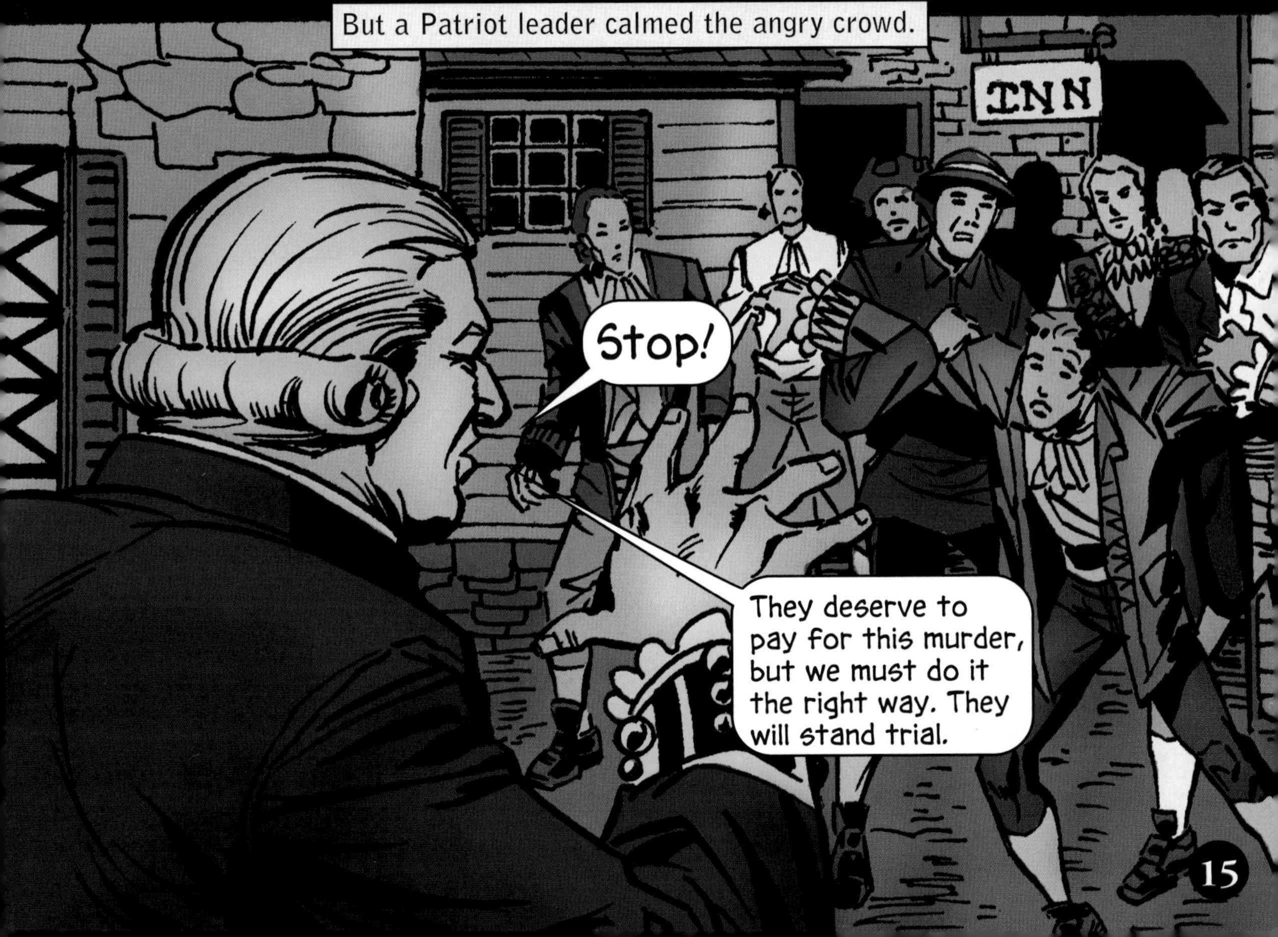
But a Patriot leader calmed the angry crowd.
INN
Stop!
They deserve to pay for this murder, but we must do it the right way. They will stand trial.

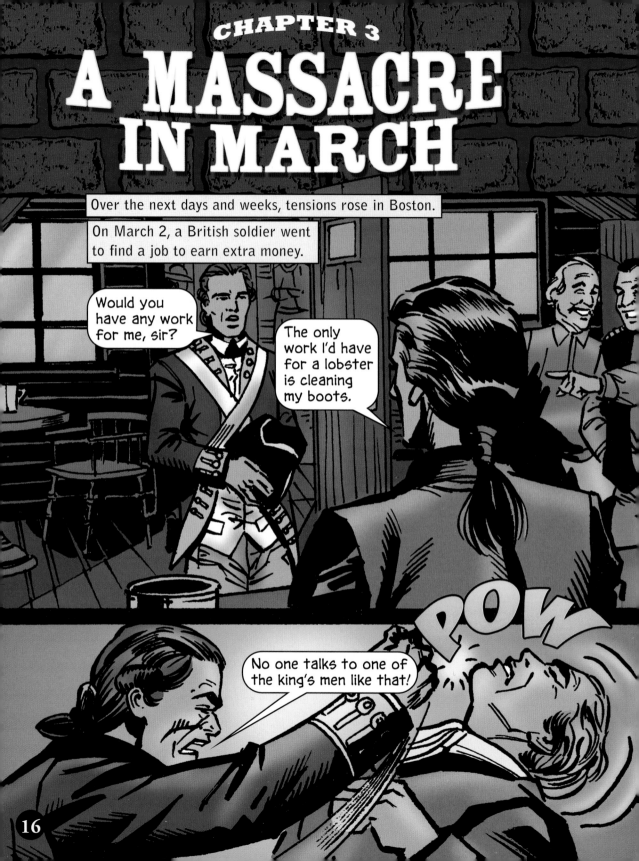

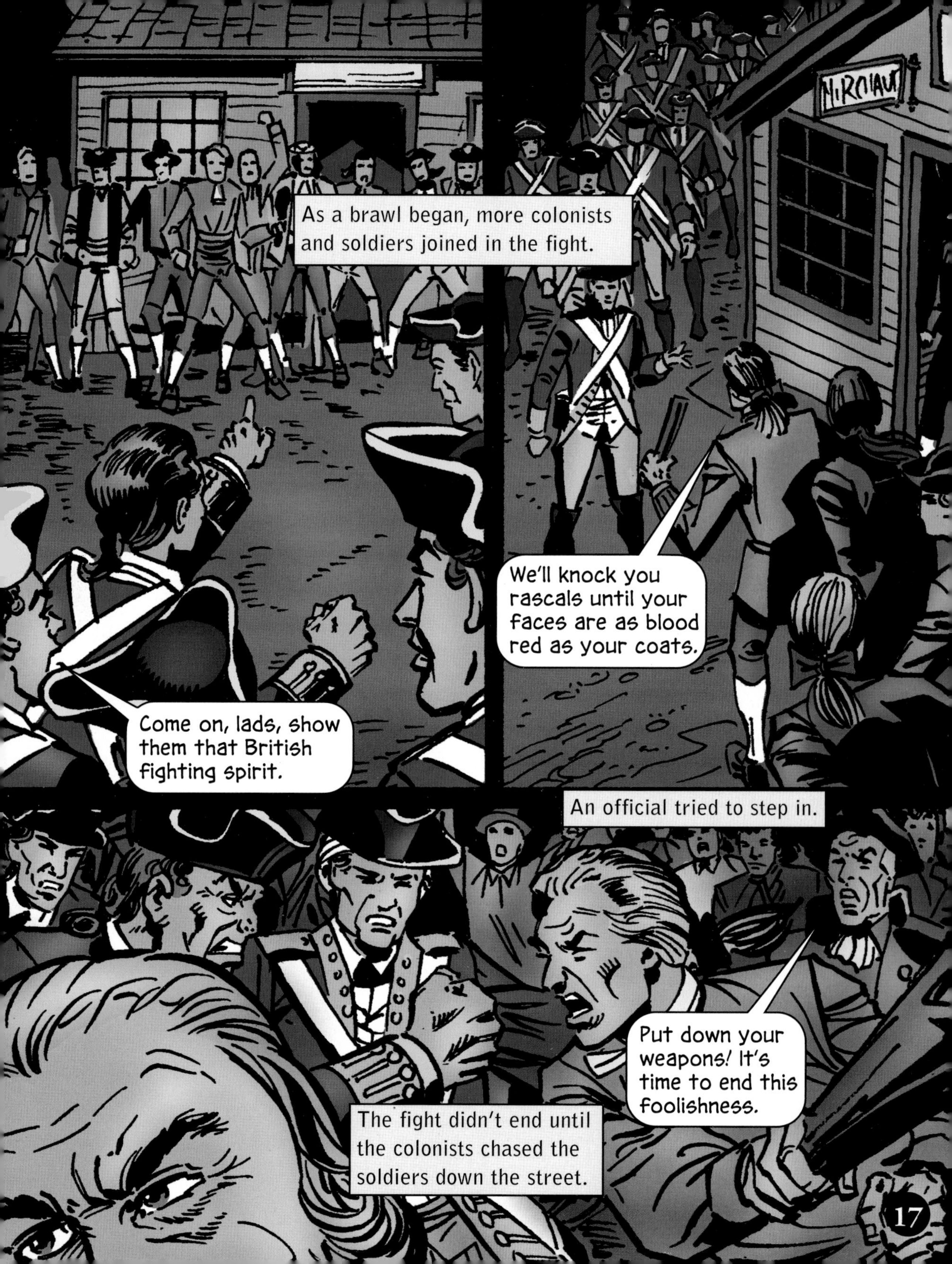
As a brawl began, more colonists and soldiers joined in the fight.
Come on, lads, show them that British fighting spirit.
We'll knock you rascals until your faces are as blood red as your coats.
An official tried to step in.
Put down your weapons! It's time to end this foolishness.
The fight didn't end until the colonists chased the soldiers down the street.

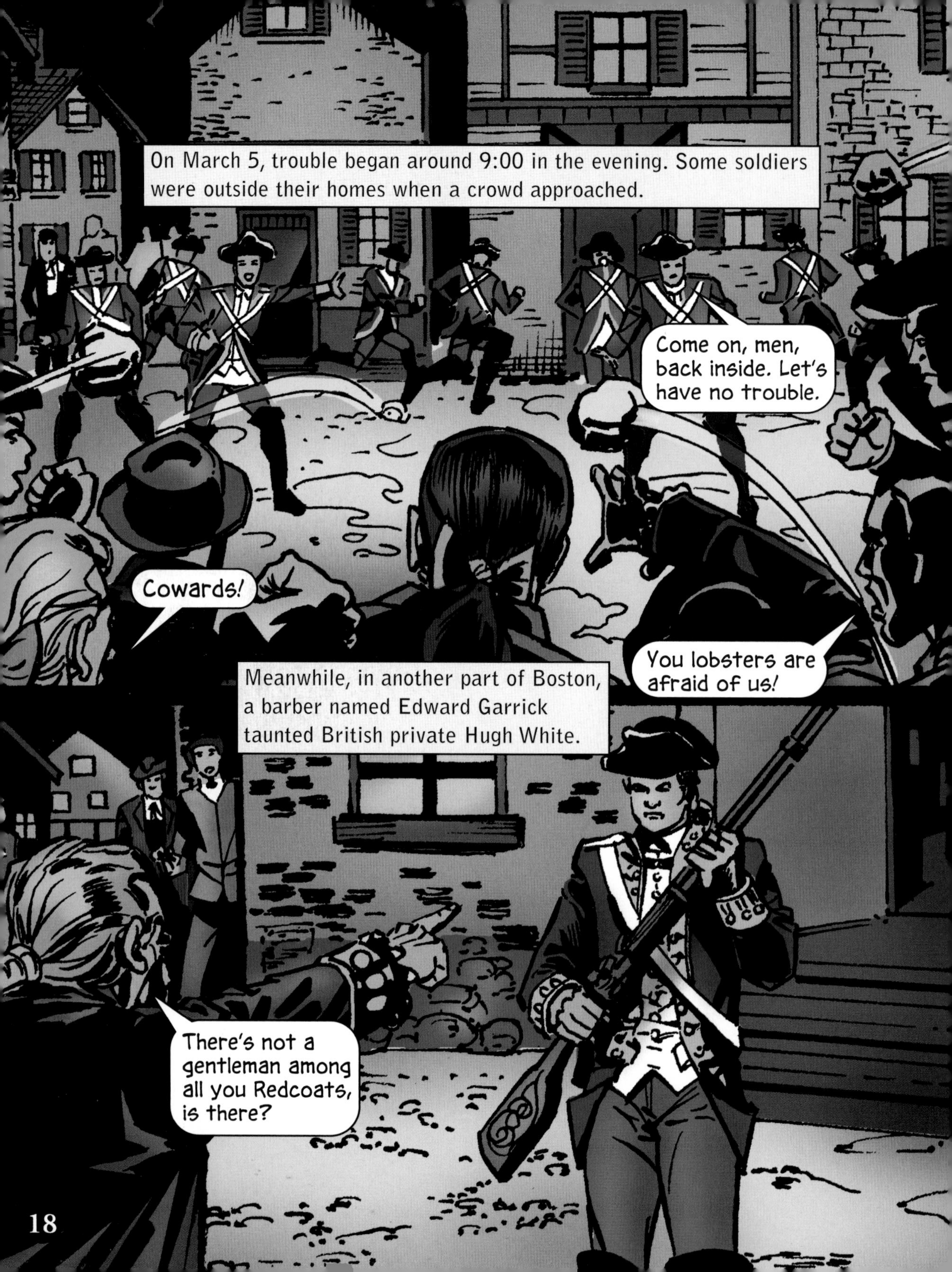

On March 5, trouble began around 9:00 in the evening. Some soldiers were outside their homes when a crowd approached.
Come on, men, back inside. Let's have no trouble.
Cowards!
You lobsters are afraid of us!
Meanwhile, in another part of Boston, a barber named Edward Garrick taunted British private Hugh White.
There's not a gentleman among all you Redcoats, is there?

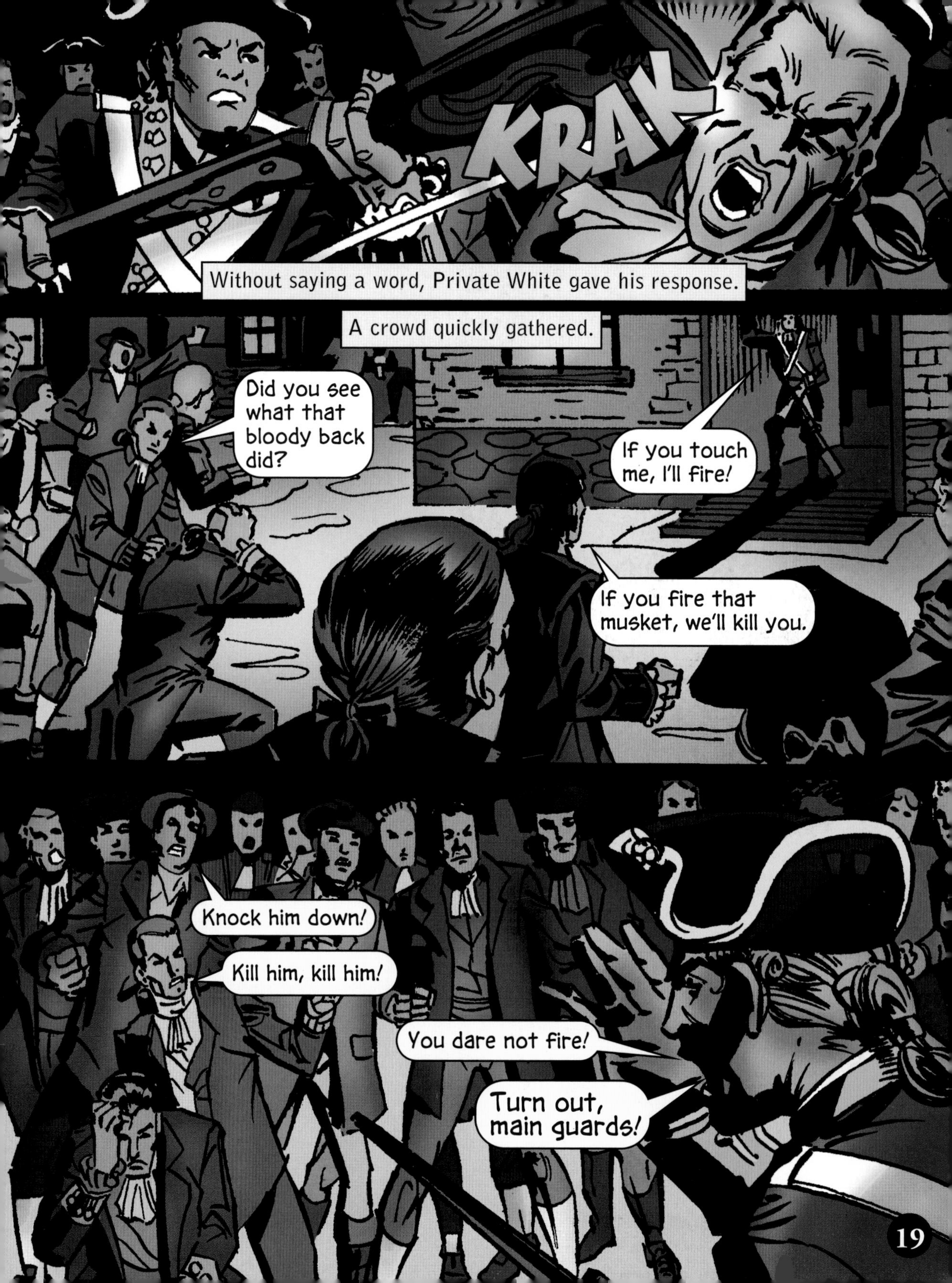
KRAK
Without saying a word, Private White gave his response.
A crowd quickly gathered.
Did you see what that bloody back did?
If you touch me, I'll fire!
If you fire that musket, we'll kill you.
Knock him down!
Kill him, kill him!
You dare not fire!
Turn out, main guards!

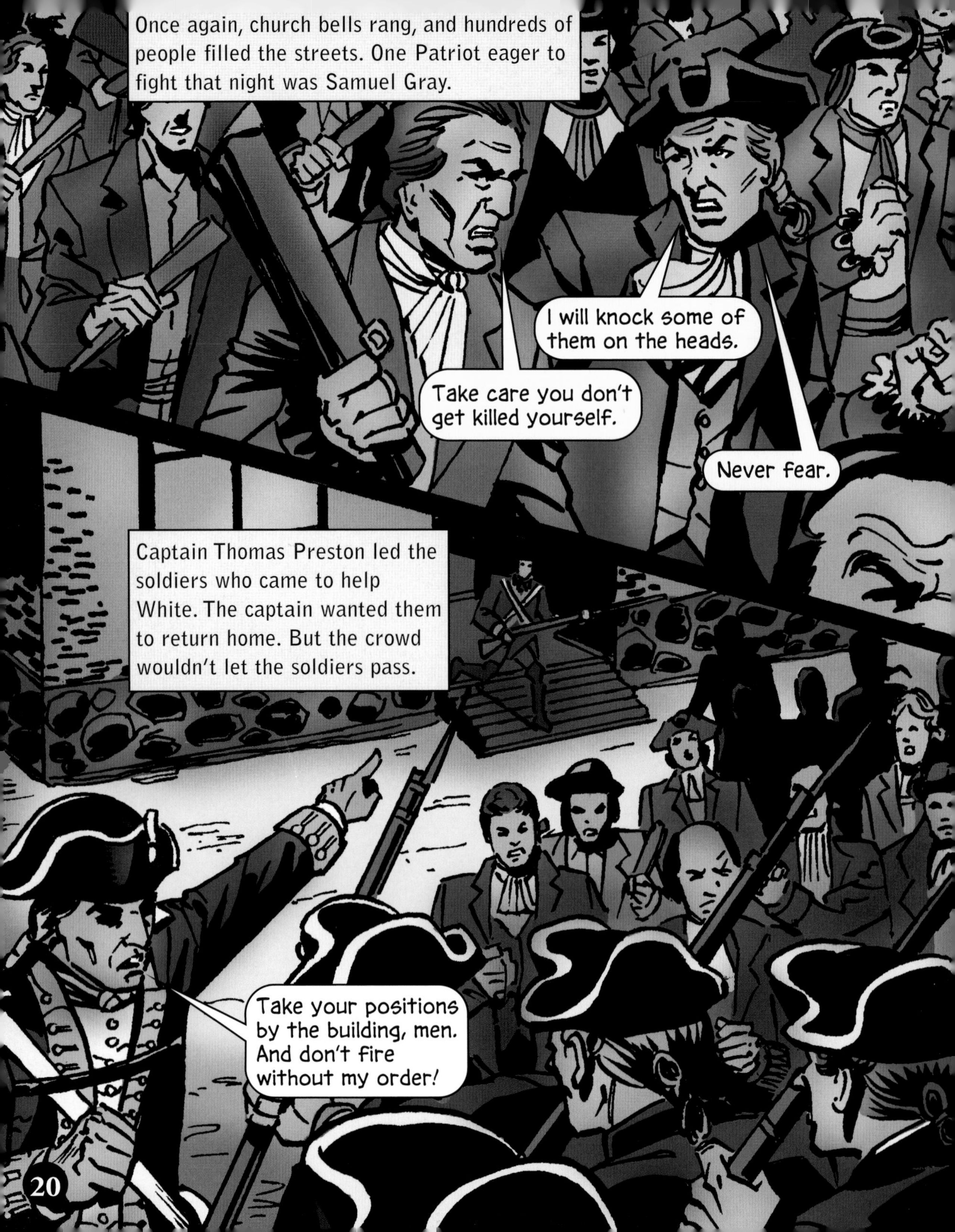
Once again, church bells rang, and hundreds of people filled the streets. One Patriot eager to fight that night was Samuel Gray.
I will knock some of them on the heads.
Take care you don't get killed yourself.
Never fear.
Captain Thomas Preston led the soldiers who came to help White. The captain wanted them to return home. But the crowd wouldn't let the soldiers pass.
Take your positions by the building, men. And don't fire without my order!

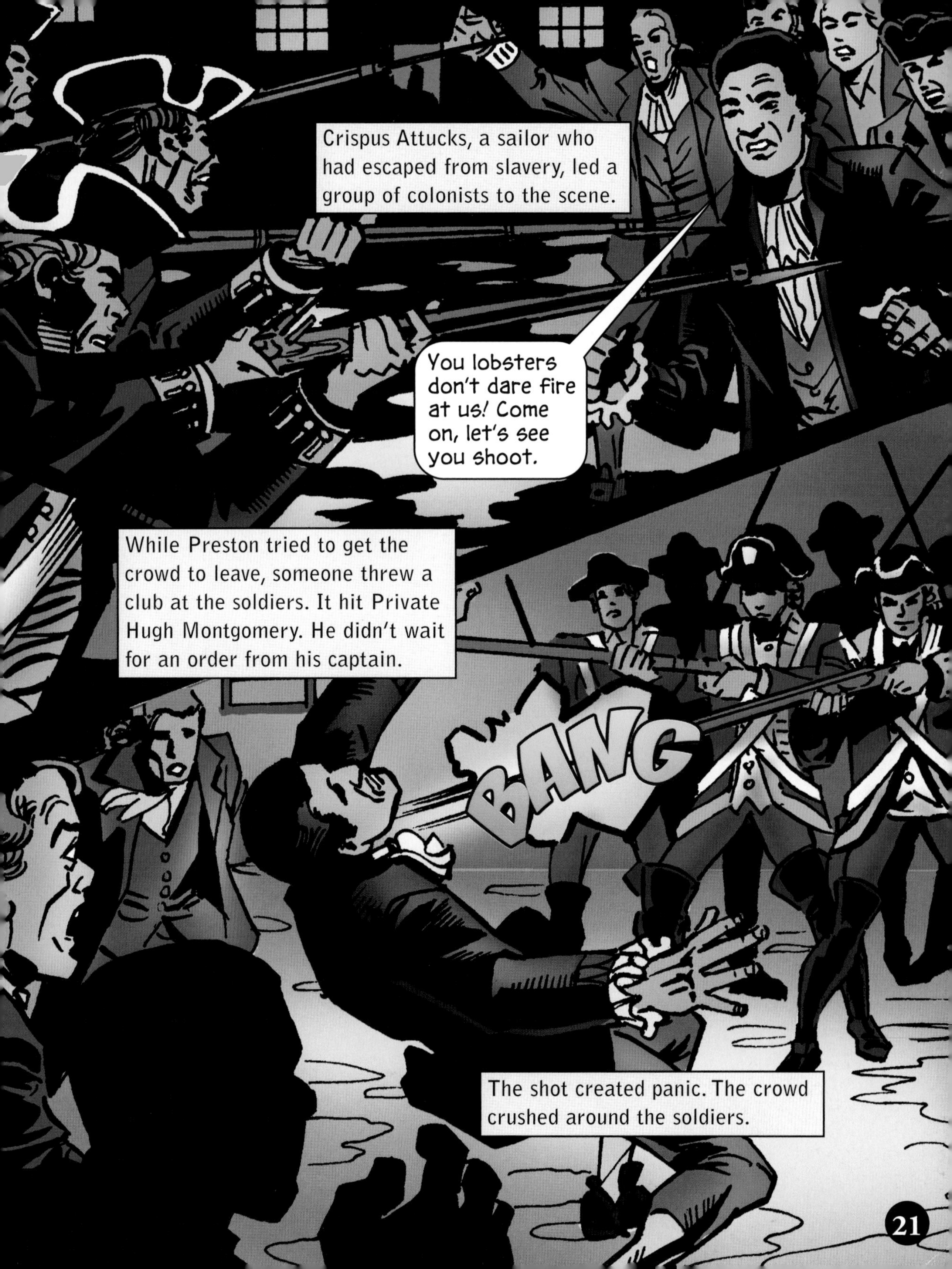
Crispus Attucks, a sailor who had escaped from slavery, led a group of colonists to the scene.
You lobsters don't dare fire at us! Come on, let's see you shoot.
While Preston tried to get the crowd to leave, someone threw a club at the soldiers. It hit Private Hugh Montgomery. He didn't wait for an order from his captain.
BANG
The shot created panic. The crowd crushed around the soldiers.

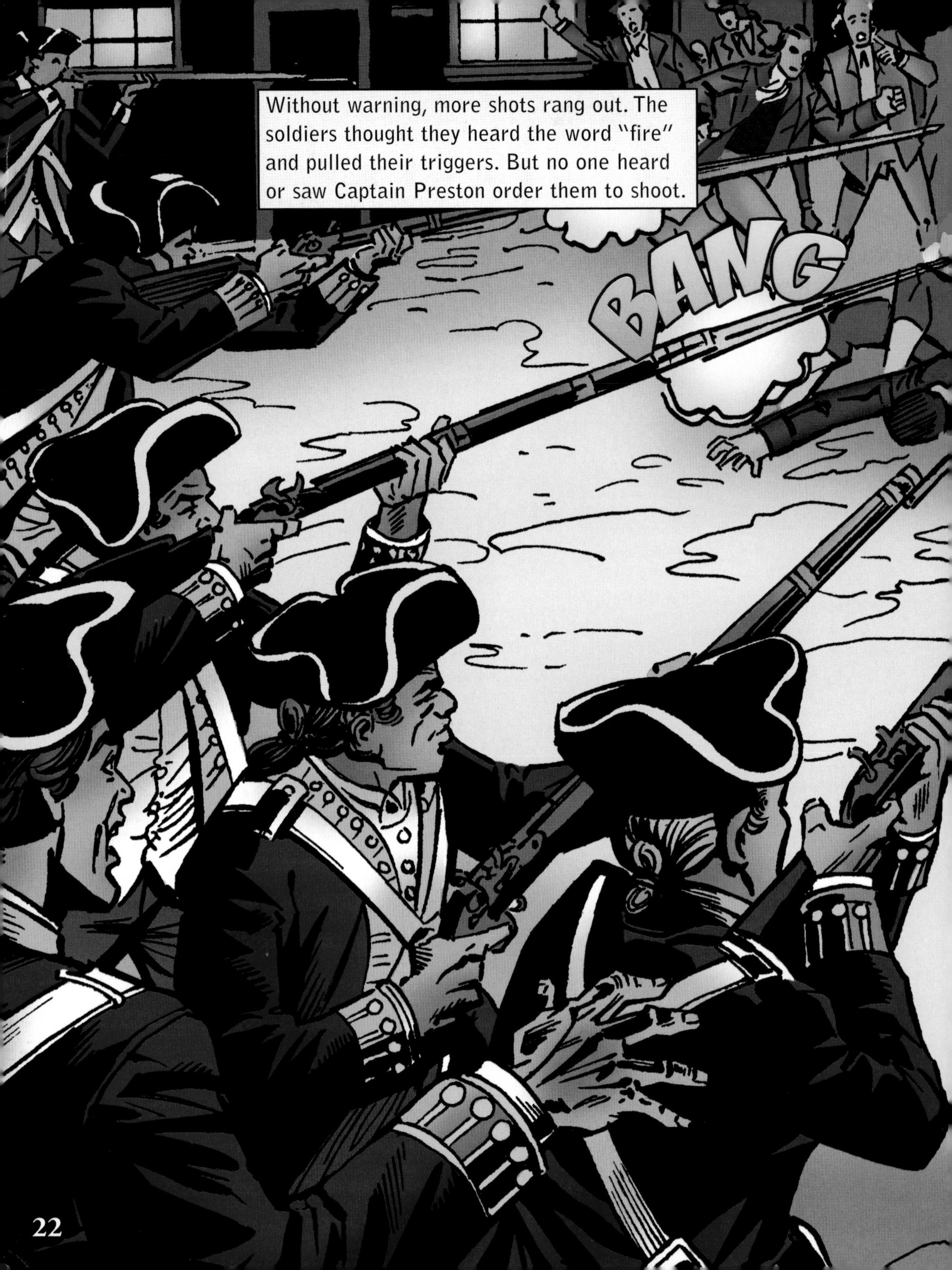
Without warning, more shots rang out. The soldiers thought they heard the word "fire" and pulled their triggers. But no one heard or saw Captain Preston order them to shoot.
BANG

CHAPTER 4
AFTER THE MASSACRE

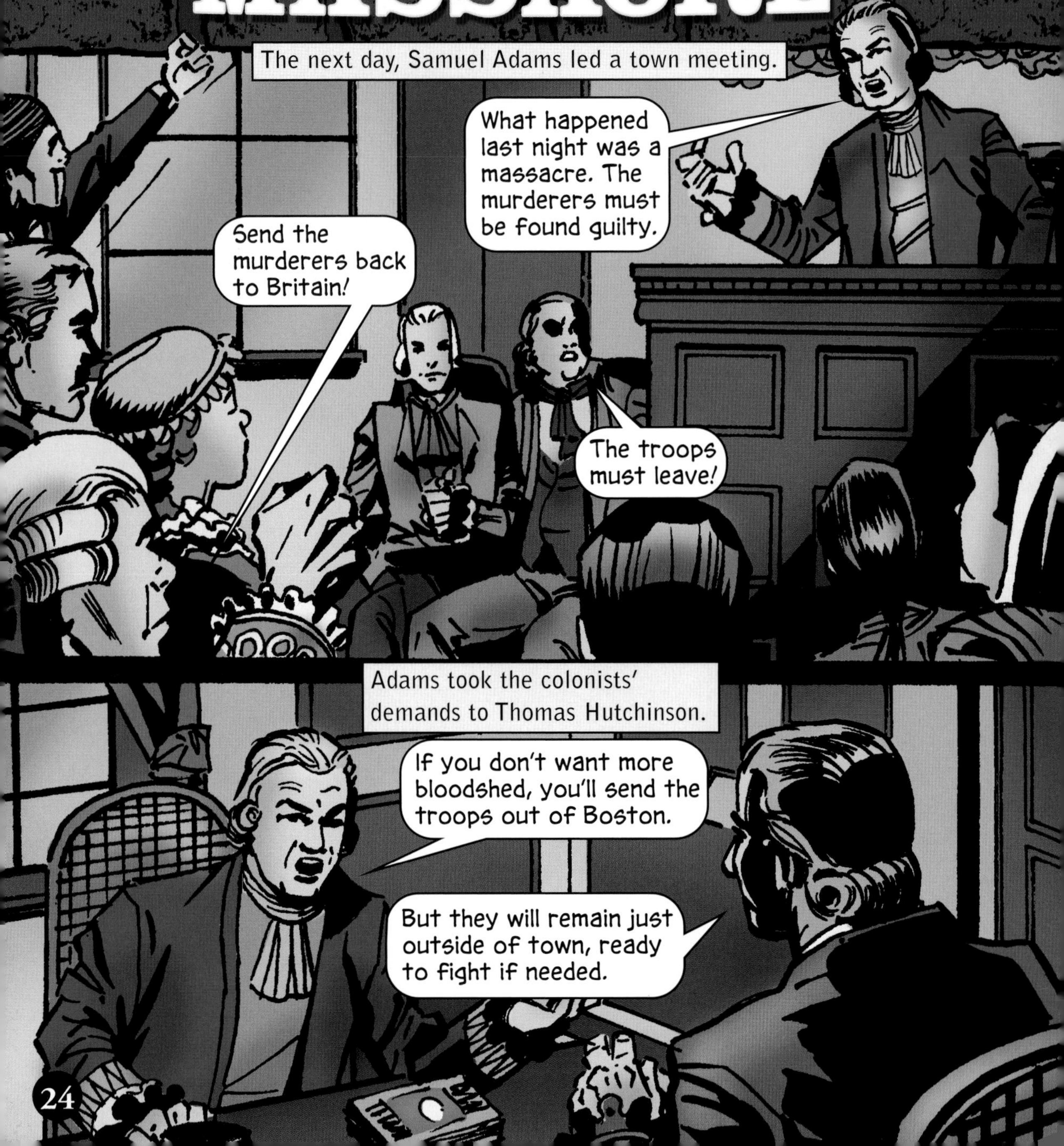

The next day, Samuel Adams led a town meeting.
What happened last night was a massacre. The murderers must be found guilty.
Send the murderers back to Britain!
The troops must leave!
Adams took the colonists' demands to Thomas Hutchinson.
If you don't want more bloodshed, you'll send the troops out of Boston.
But they will remain just outside of town, ready to fight if needed.

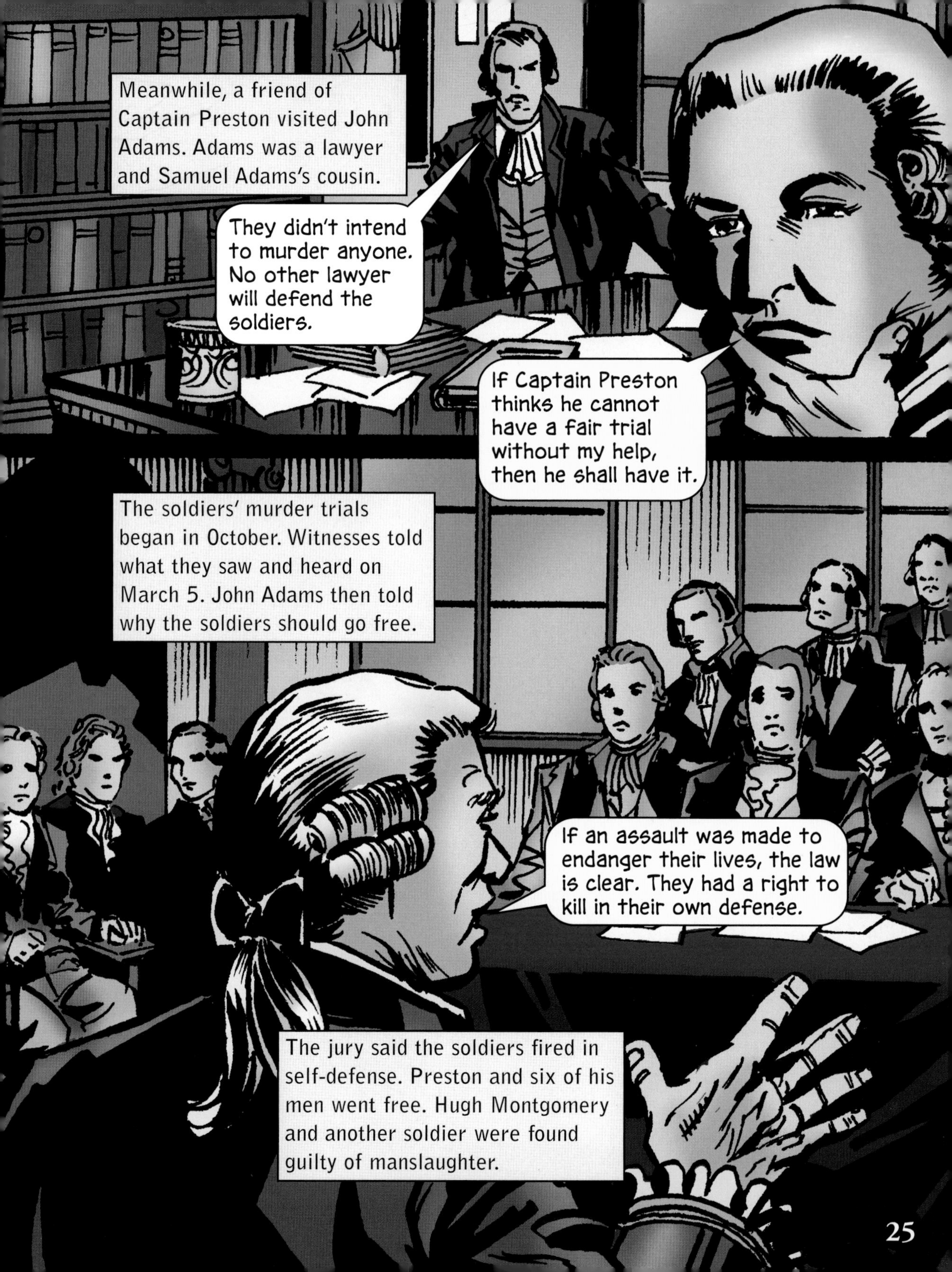
Meanwhile, a friend of Captain Preston visited John Adams. Adams was a lawyer and Samuel Adams's cousin.
They didn't intend to murder anyone. No other lawyer will defend the soldiers.
If Captain Preston thinks he cannot have a fair trial without my help, then he shall have it.
The soldiers' murder trials began in October. Witnesses told what they saw and heard on March 5. John Adams then told why the soldiers should go free.
If an assault was made to endanger their lives, the law is clear. They had a right to kill in their own defense.
The jury said the soldiers fired in self-defense. Preston and six of his men went free. Hugh Montgomery and another soldier were found guilty of manslaughter.

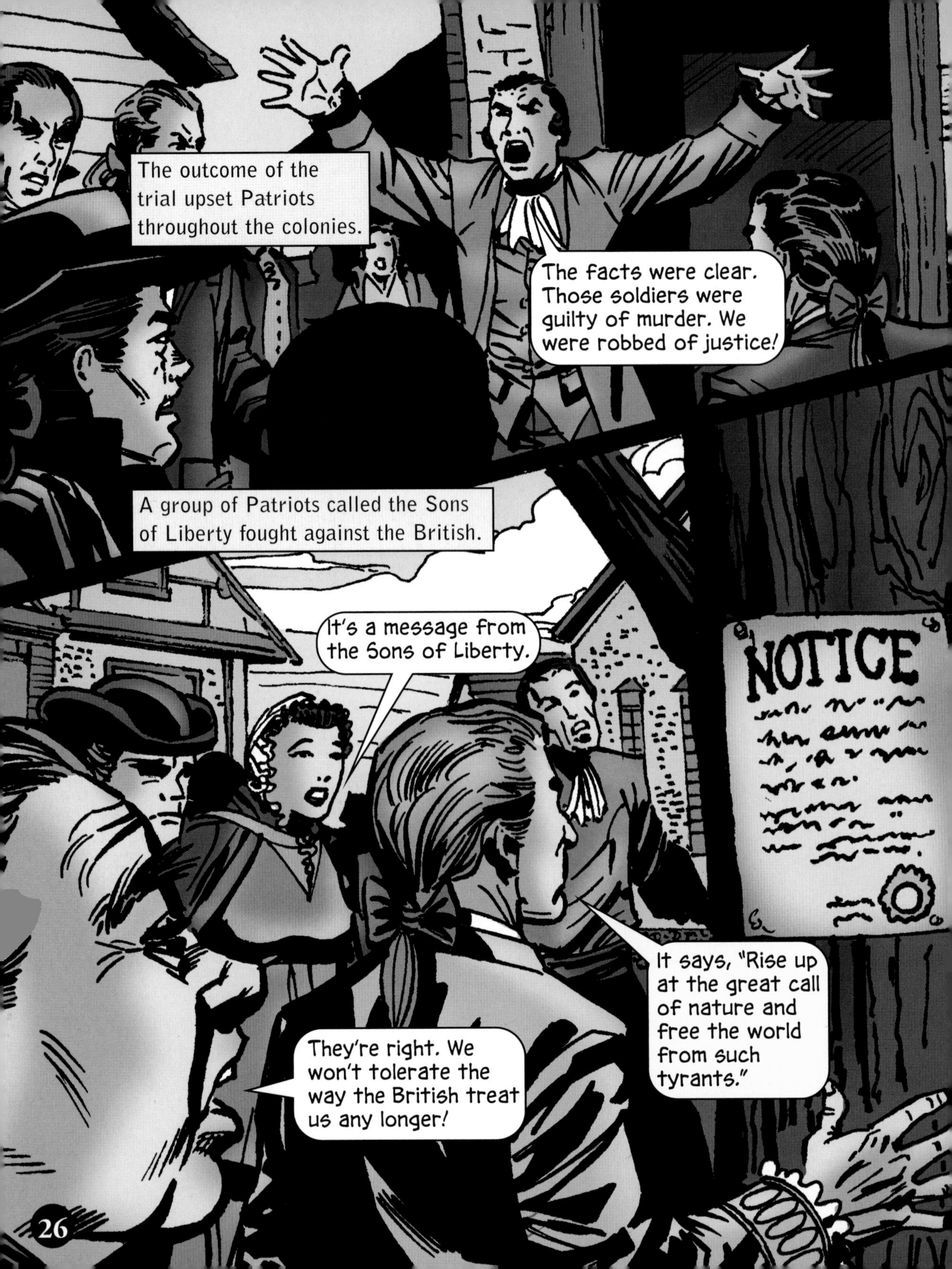
The outcome of the trial upset Patriots throughout the colonies.
The facts were clear. Those soldiers were guilty of murder. We were robbed of justice!
A group of Patriots called the Sons of Liberty fought against the British.
It's a message from the Sons of Liberty.
NOTICE
It says, "Rise up at the great call of nature and free the world from such tyrants."
They're right. We won't tolerate the way the British treat us any longer!

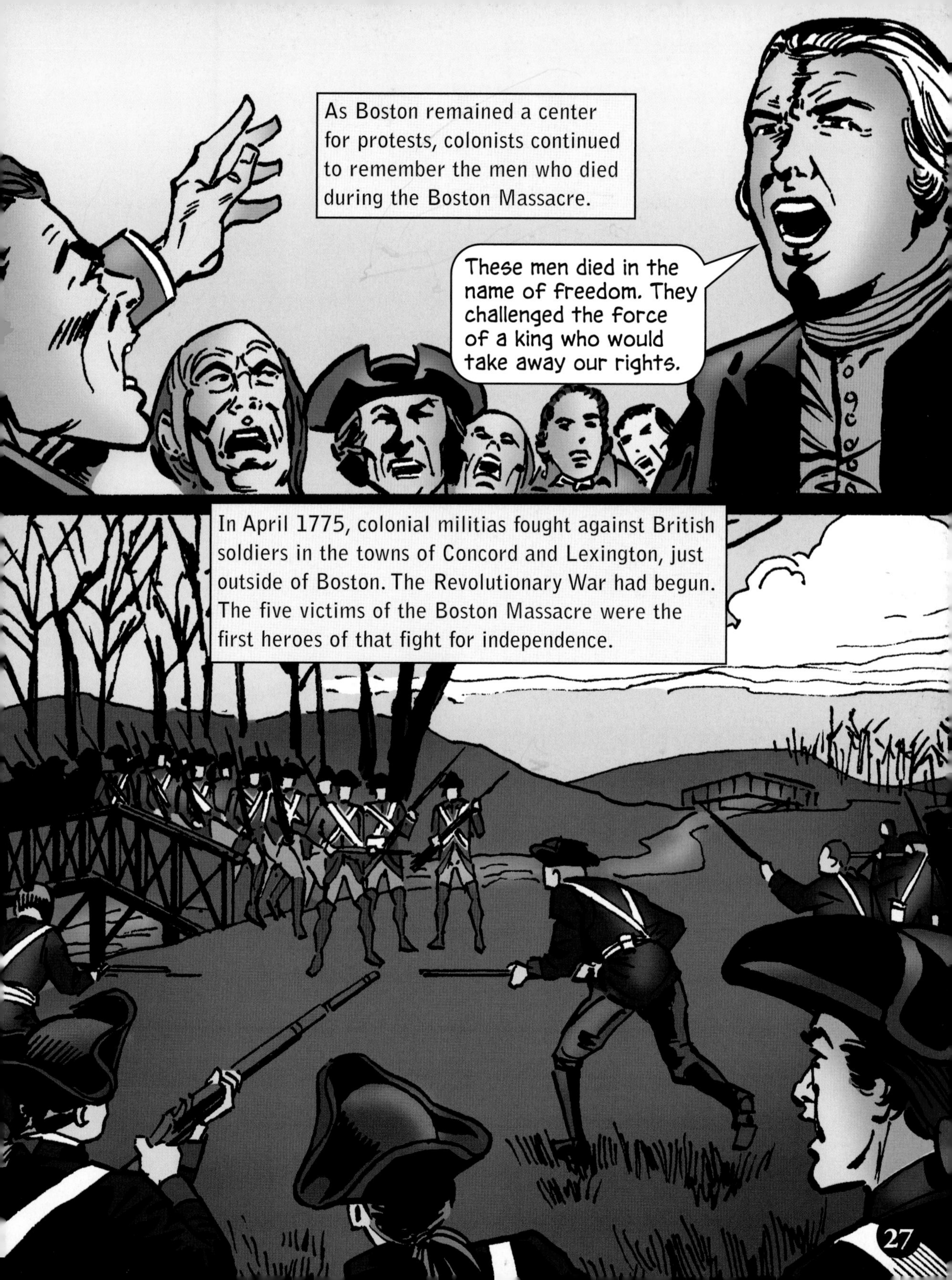
As Boston remained a center for protests, colonists continued to remember the men who died during the Boston Massacre.
These men died in the name of freedom. They challenged the force of a king who would take away our rights.
In April 1775, colonial militias fought against British soldiers in the towns of Concord and Lexington, just outside of Boston. The Revolutionary War had begun. The five victims of the Boston Massacre were the first heroes of that fight for independence.

MORE ABOUT THE
BOSTON
MASSACRE

- Crispus Attucks was the first man to die in the Boston Massacre. He was part Native American and part African American. A statue honoring Attucks stands in Boston Common, the largest park in Boston.

- The other victims of the Boston Massacre were Samuel Gray, Samuel Maverick, Patrick Carr, and James Caldwell. Maverick died the day after the massacre, and Carr died several days later.

- British soldiers Hugh Montgomery and Matthew Kilroy were found guilty of manslaughter for the deaths of Crispus Attucks and Samuel Gray. They could have been executed for their crime. Under British law, however, they were allowed to ask for special treatment. Instead of being killed, each man had a mark burned onto his right thumb with a hot iron.

- After the Boston Massacre, Samuel and John Adams continued to play important roles in America's struggle for independence. Both wrote important articles explaining how British policies hurt the colonies. Samuel was one of the first Patriot leaders to call for independence. John later became the second president of the United States.

- In colonial times, British law did not allow gatherings of more than 12 people in the streets. By reading aloud a law called the Riot Act, a British official could break up the crowd. If people didn't leave after the Riot Act was read, soldiers could fire into the crowd. Colonists on the streets of Boston thought they were safe the night of March 5, 1770. No one had read the Riot Act when the troops arrived.

- A marker in Boston's Granary Burying Ground shows where the five victims of the Boston Massacre are buried. Eleven-year-old Christopher Seider is also buried there. His last name is incorrectly spelled "Snider" on the tombstone. Samuel Adams is also buried near these graves.

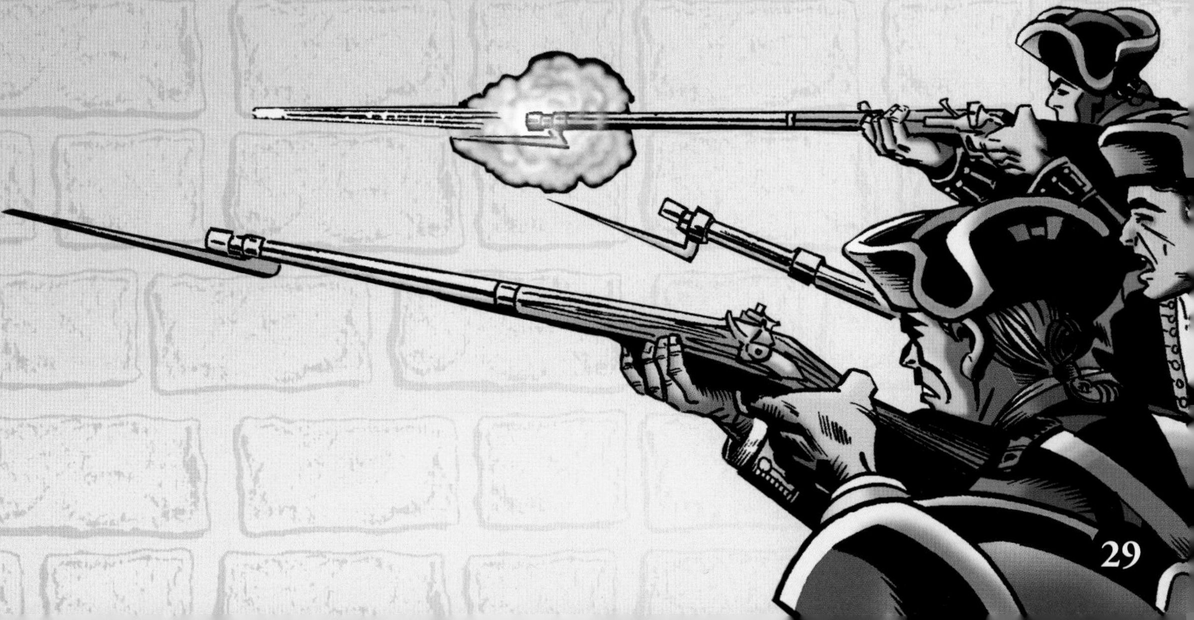

GLOSSARY

bayonet (BAY-uh-net)—a long metal blade attached to the end of a rifle

boycott (BOI-kot)—to refuse to buy something as a way of making a protest

import (IM-port)—to bring goods into a place or country from elsewhere

Loyalist (LOI-uh-list)—a colonist who was loyal to Great Britain before and during the Revolutionary War

manslaughter (MAN-slaw-tur)—the crime of killing someone without intending to do so

massacre (MASS-uh-kur)—the killing of a large number of people, often in battle

Parliament (PAR-luh-muhnt)—the governing body that makes the laws in Britain

Patriot (PAY-tree-uht)—a person who sided with the colonies before and during the Revolutionary War

smuggle (SMUHG-uhl)—to bring something in or out of a country illegally

INTERNET SITES

FactHound offers a safe, fun way to find Internet sites related to this book. All of the sites on FactHound have been researched by our staff.

Here's how:

1. Visit *www.facthound.com*
2. Type in this special code **073684368X** for age-appropriate sites. Or enter a search word related to this book for a more general search.
3. Click on the **Fetch It** button.

FactHound will fetch the best sites for you!

READ MORE

Draper, Allison Stark. *The Boston Massacre: Five Colonists Killed by British Soldiers.* Headlines from History. New York: PowerKids Press, 2001.

Mattern, Joanne. *The Cost of Freedom: Crispus Attucks and the Boston Massacre.* Great Moments in American History. New York: Rosen, 2003.

Ready, Dee. *The Boston Massacre.* Let Freedom Ring. Mankato, Minn.: Bridgestone Books, 2002.

Santella, Andrew. *The Boston Massacre.* Cornerstones of Freedom. New York: Children's Press, 2004.

BIBLIOGRAPHY

The Boston Historical Society and Museum
http://rfi.bostonhistory.org/

Boston Massacre Historical Society
http://www.bostonmassacre.net/

The Boston Massacre Trial of 1770
http://www.law.umkc.edu/faculty/projects/ftrials/bostonmassacre/bostonmassacre.html

Fleming, Thomas. *Liberty!: The American Revolution.* New York: Viking, 1997.

Langguth, A. J. *Patriots: The Men Who Started the American Revolution.* New York: Simon & Schuster, 1988.

Zobel, Hiller B. *The Boston Massacre.* New York: W. W. Norton, 1970.

INDEX